Sunshine

Activity Book 3

Class 3

EARLY START EDITION

Cornelsen

Contents

Hello again		4
Unit 1	Meeting friends	5
Unit 2	Pets in the garden	11
Unit 3	At school	17
Unit 4	The second-hand shop	23
Unit 5	Free-time activities	29
Unit 6	In the park	35
Unit 7	Special days	41
Word fields		49
Cut-out-pages		53

Symbols

CD 1.9
listen to the CD · CD 1 track 9

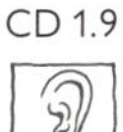
listen

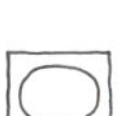
speak

read

play

write

What's your name?

1 Read the texts.

2 Fill in the speech bubble.

3 Draw yourself.

4 What English words do you know? Write the words.

What have they got?

CD 1.7
1 Listen to the CD. Draw lines.

2 Read the words.

3 Complete the speech bubbles.

bike · scooter
mountain bike
skateboard

4 Complete the sentences.

Harry's · Kate's · Emily's · Samir's

1 It's ______________ skateboard. 

2 It's ______________ ____________________

3 It's ______________ ____________________

4 It's ______________ ____________________ 

Numbers

CD 1.12

1 Listen to the CD. Write the phone numbers.

CD 1.12

2 Listen to the CD. Draw lines.

1 2 3 4

3 Harry and Kate are playing hopscotch. Write the words.

Telefonnummern verstehen, Zahlen lesen (S.75)

Colours

1 Listen. Colour the things.

2 Complete the sentences.

blue · green · orange
pink · red · yellow

1 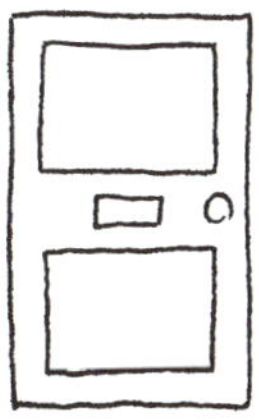

It's a ____________ door.

2 

It's a ____________ bike.

3 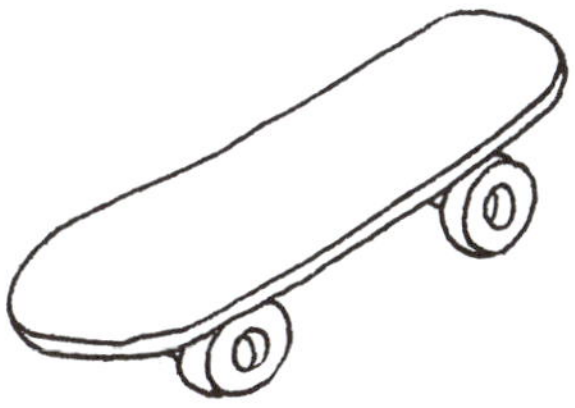

It's a ____________ skateboard.

4 

____________ house.

5 

____________ T-shirt.

6 

____________ scooter.

3 Do a colour dictation.

How are you?

1 Write what the children are saying.

2 How are you? Write your answer.

I'm fine, thank you.
I'm OK.
I'm not so well.

Portfolio: About me

1 What's your name?

My name is ______________________________

2 What are your friends' names?

My friends' names are ______________________________

____

3 How old are you?

I'm ______________________________

4 What's your phone number?

My phone number is ______________________________

5 What toys have you got?

I've got ______________________________

____

6 What's your favourite colour?

My favourite colour is

____

Check your English

Ich fand die Aufgabe: ☺ leicht ☹ mittel ☹ schwer

CD 1.14

1 ☐ ☐ ☐ ☐ ☐ ☐ ☐ ☐ ☐ ☐

Ich habe ______ Zahlen verstanden und aufgeschrieben. (✓) ☐

2 Ich habe zwei Kinder nach ihrer Telefonnummer gefragt.
Ich habe die Nummern wiederholt. (✓) ☐

______________________ : ______________________
Name

______________________ : ______________________
Name

3 Ich habe die folgenden Zahlen geschrieben. (✓) ☐

2 8 11 4

__________ __________ __________ __________

4 Ich habe mit (Name) ______________________ ein Farbdiktat durchgeführt. (✓) ☐

1 ______________ 2 ______________ 3 ______________

4 ______________ 5 ______________ 6 ______________

Ich habe geprüft, ob ich die Farbwörter richtig geschrieben habe. (✓) ☐

5 Ich habe (Name) ______________________ nach seiner/ihrer Lieblingsfarbe gefragt. (✓) ☐

Feed your pets

CD 1.15

1 Listen to the CD. Point to the right picture.

2 Say the chant.

Please drink your milk and eat your bread.
Yes, Mum. Yes.

Please feed your dog in the garden shed.
Yes, Dad. Yes.

CD 1.15

3 Listen to the CD. Number the pictures.

4 Write the animal words.

dog · rabbit · rat

☐ ____________

☐ ____________

☐ ____________

At the pet shop

CD 1.20

1 Listen to the CD. Number the pet foods.

2 Write the words.

3 Play the game.

cat · dog
guinea pig · hamster
rabbit · rat

Bilder nummerieren, Wörter lesen und schreiben (S. 89) · ein Spiel spielen (S. 90)

Rabbit's party

CD 1.22

1 Listen to the CD. Number the pets.

CD 1.22

2 Listen to the CD. Tick the right food.

3 Write the words for the pets.

4 Complete the speech bubbles.

apples · carrots · guinea pig · lettuce
peanuts · rabbit · rat · hamster

Pets and food

1 Read the words in the box.

2 Look at the pictures. Number the words in the box.

3 Write the words in the puzzle.

2 apple	☐ carrot	☐ cat	☐ dog	☐ guinea pig
☐ hamster	☐ lettuce	☐ peanuts	☐ rabbit	☐ rat

4 Write the words.

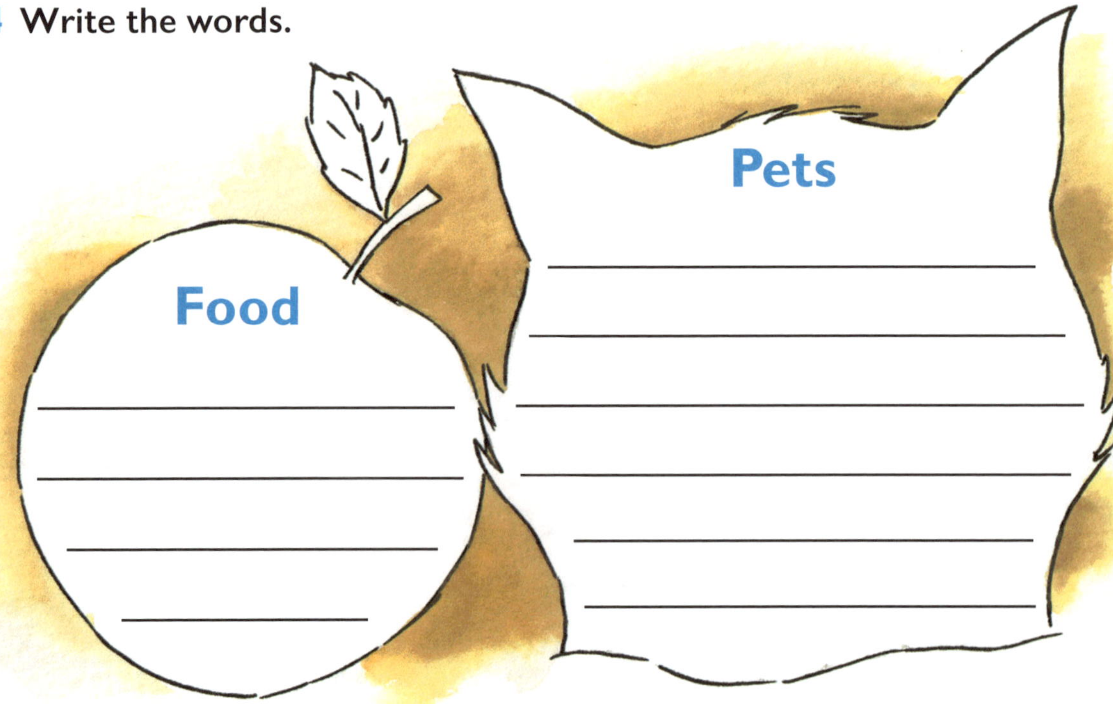

Portfolio: My pets

1 What pets do you like?

I like ______________________________

____

2 Have you got a pet?

Yes, I have. · No, I haven't.

____

3 Write about your pet.

I've got ______________________________

My pet's name is ______________________________

My pet's favourite food: ______________________________

____

What colour is your pet? ______________________________

____

Here's a picture of my pet.

Check your English

Ich fand die Aufgabe: ☺ leicht 😐 mittel ☹ schwer

1 Ich habe (Name) ____________________ die *chants* *Drink your milk* und *Drink your tea* vorgetragen. ☐

2 Ich habe (Name) ____________________ am Telefon zum Spielen eingeladen. ☐

3 Ich habe (Name) ____________________ gesagt, wie diese Tiere heißen. ☐

 ☐  ☐  ☐

____________ ____________ ____________

 ☐  ☐  ☐

____________ ____________ ____________

Ich habe ________ Wörter richtig geschrieben.

4 Ich kenne noch mehr Tierwörter. ☐

____

5 Ich habe (Name) ____________________ etwas über mein Haustier erzählt. ☐

What's in your school bag?

CD 1.25

1 Listen to the CD. Number the pictures.

2 Colour your school things. Talk to your partner.

My school things

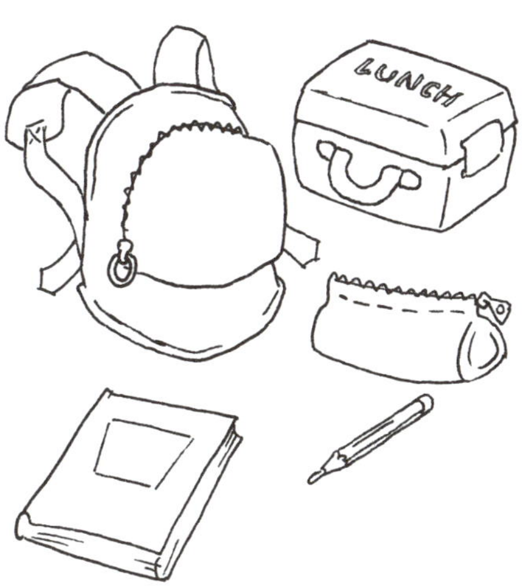

My partner's school things

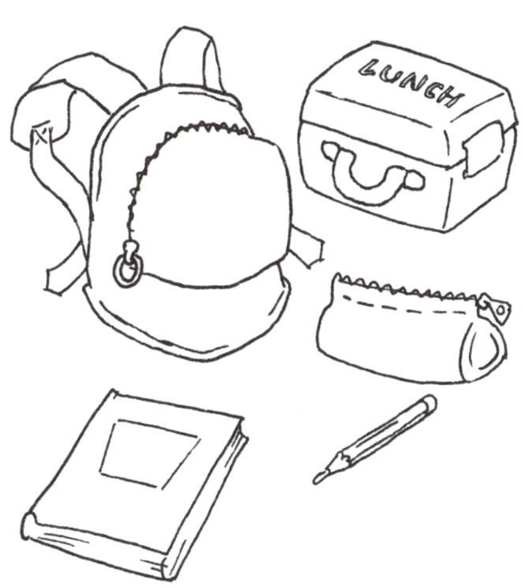

School things

1 Read the sentences. How many school things are there?

two · three · four · five
six · felt tips · lunch boxes
pencil cases · school bags

2 Complete the sentences.

There are five pencils.

There are _______ books.

There are _______ rulers.

There are ________ rubbers.

There are ____________________.

There ________________________________.

____.

____.

3 What's missing? Write the words.

Sätze lesen, Wörter und Sätze schreiben (S.106)

What we do at school

1 Read the sentences. Draw lines.

1

2

Read the text in the book.

Draw a lunch box.

Write your name.

Colour the lunch box red.

3

4

2 Listen to the CD. Number the pictures.

CD 1.30

Asking for school things

CD 1.31

1 What has Kate got? Listen to the CD. Tick or cross out.

2 What are the children saying? Fill in the speech bubbles.

glue stick · pencil sharpener · ruler · scissors

Einen Hörtext verstehen (S.111) · Sätze zu Bildern ergänzen (S.112)

Portfolio: A picture story

1 Cut out the speech bubbles on page 55. Complete the story.

2 Read the story with a partner.

Check your English

Ich fand die Aufgabe: ☺ leicht ☺ mittel ☹ schwer

1 Ich habe (Name) ______________________ den *chant* *Books in your school bag?* vorgetragen. ☐

2

CD 1.32

☐ ☐ ☐ ☐ ☐ ☐ ☐ ☐

Ich habe ______ Gegenstände richtig nummeriert.

3 Ich habe (Name) ______________________ gesagt, welche der oben abgebildeten Dinge ich in meiner Federmappe habe und welche nicht. ☐

4

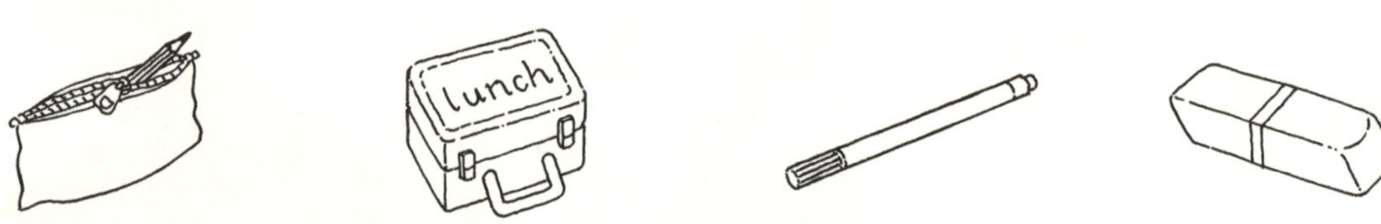

Ich habe mit (Name) ______________________ ein Farbdiktat durchgeführt. ☐

5 (Name) ______________________ und ich haben eine Geschichte mit verteilten Rollen gelesen (Seite 21). ☐

What are they wearing?

CD 1.33

1 Listen to the CD. Colour the children's clothes.

2 Complete the sentences.

black · blue
brown · green
grey · orange
red · yellow
gloves · hat
jacket · shoes

1 Harry is wearing ________________ and a ____________.

2 Kate is wearing a ______________ and ________________.

3 Samir is wearing a _____________ and ________________.

4 Emily is wearing _____________ and a ______________.

3 Say the words. Draw what's next.

Clothes

1 Write the words.

coat · dress
gloves · hat
jacket
pullover · scarf
shirt · skirt
shoes
trousers

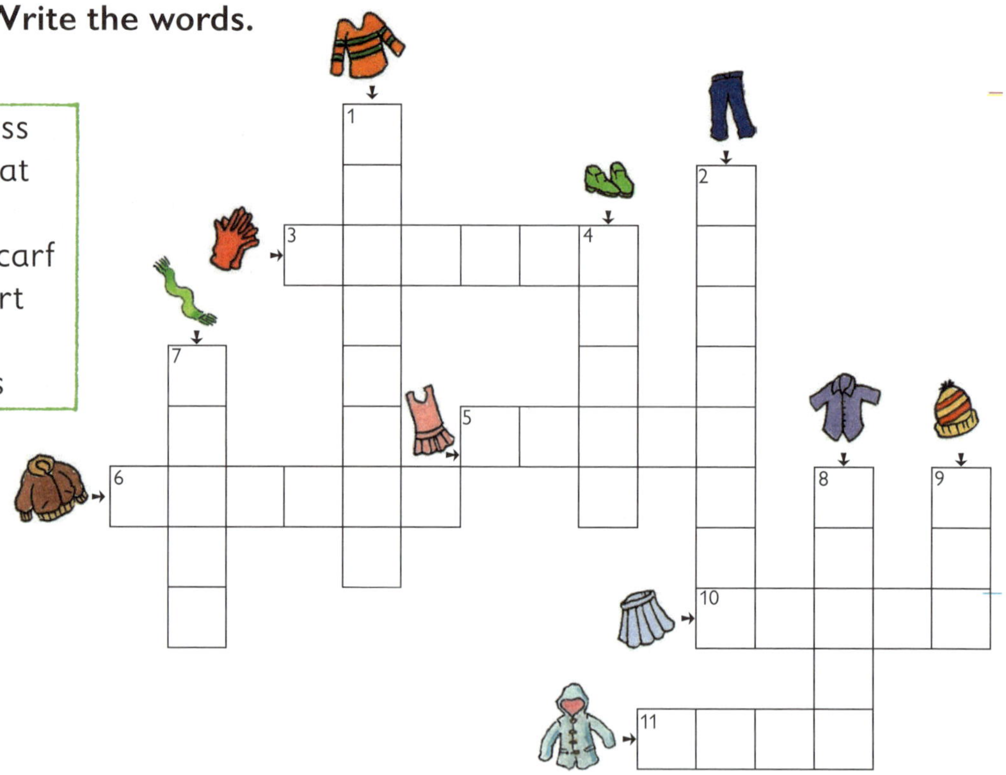

2 Write the missing words. Tick your answer.

1

Do you like the ______________?

☐ Yes, I do.
☐ No, I don't.

2

Do you like the ______________?

☐ Yes, I do.
☐ No, I don't.

3

Do you like the ______________?

☐ Yes, I do.
☐ No, I don't.

4

____
______________________?

☐ Yes, I do.
☐ No, I don't.

Ein Kreuzworträtsel lösen, Fragen vervollständigen und beantworten (S.126)

A game

trousers jacket pullover gloves hat shoes

1 **Write the words.**

2 **Play the game.**

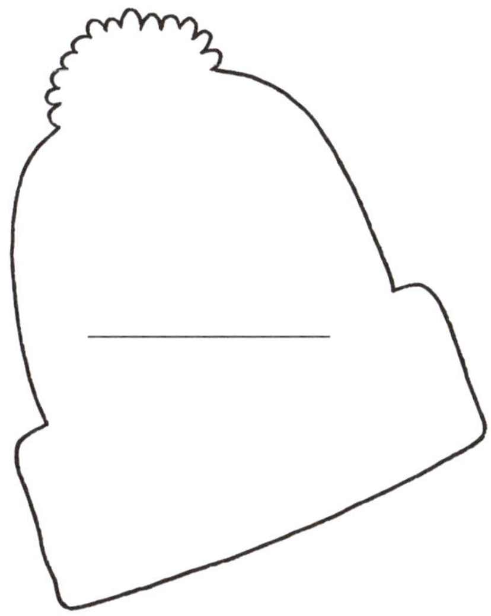

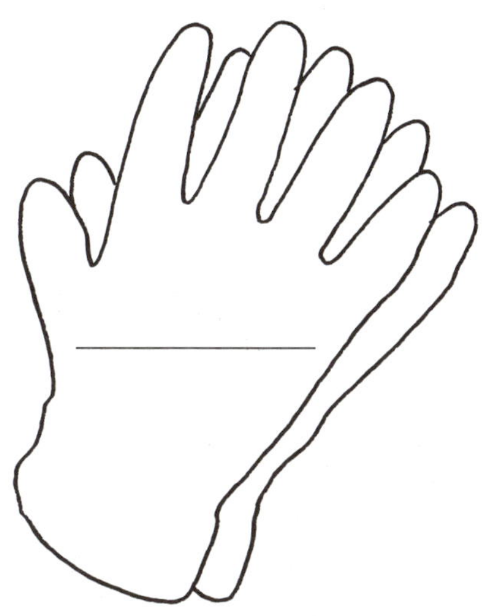

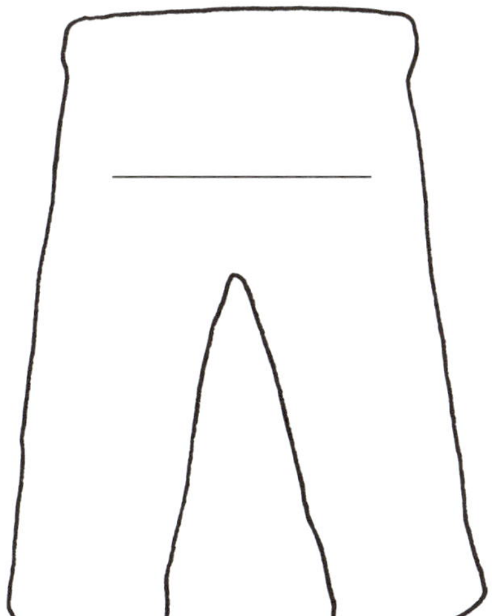

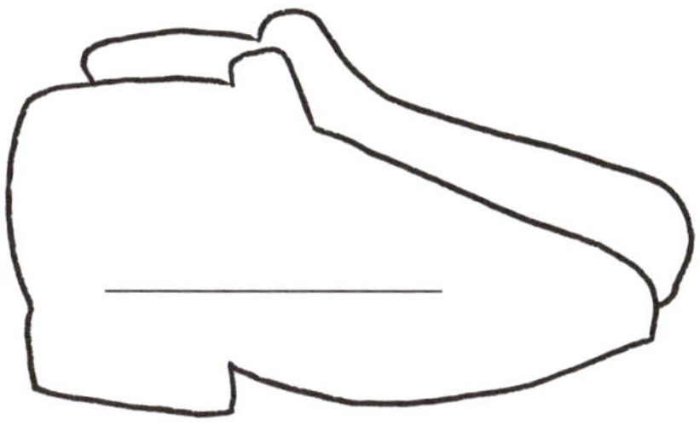

A funny boy

CD 1.40

1 Listen to the story. What's the boy wearing? Draw the lines.

too small

too big

2 Count the clothes. Complete the sentences.

dresses · hats · pullovers · shirts · shoes

 There are ____________________

 There are ____________________

 There are ____________________

 ____________________

 ____________________

Portfolio: My favourite clothes

☐ at a party ☐ at school ☐ ____________________

Here I'm wearing

____

____

____

Check your English

Ich fand die Aufgabe: ☺ leicht 😐 mittel ☹ schwer

1 CD 1.41

☐ ☐ ☐ ☐ ☐ ☐

Ich habe ______ Kleidungsstücke richtig nummeriert.

Zwei Bilder sind übrig geblieben: __________ und __________ .
Ich habe geprüft, ob ich die Wörter richtig geschrieben habe. ☐

2 Ich habe mit (Name) ____________________ das Lied *If you're happy* gesungen. ☐

3

________________ ________________
________________ ________________
________________ ________________

Ich habe geprüft, ob ich die Wörter richtig geschrieben habe. ☐

4 (Name) ____________________ und ich haben einander gefragt, ob uns die Kleidungsstücke auf den Bildkarten gefallen. ☐

5 Ich habe (Name) ____________________ gezeigt, was ich gerne anziehe, und habe vorgelesen, was ich dazu geschrieben habe (Seite 27). ☐

Do you like reading?

CD 2.5

1 Listen to the CD. Find the right answers.

2 Ask two boys and two girls about their activities. Write their names. Tick their activities.

Do you like listening to music?

Yes, I do.

No, I don't.

Names	listening to music	meeting friends	playing computer games	playing football	reading	watching TV

What we like doing

1 Read the words.

2 Write the words.

listening to music · meeting friends
playing computer games
playing football · reading · watching TV

3 Listen to the CD. Draw the lines.

CD 2.6

4 Listen to your teacher. Number the pictures.

Rooms

1 **Write the words.**

2 **Draw pictures. Tell a partner what's in the rooms.**

bath · bathroom · bed · bedroom desk · kitchen · lamp · living room · oven sofa · table · toilet · TV · wardrobe	a book · a cat · a football a hat · a rat · a school bag shoes · a skateboard

Sagen, was sich in den Räumen befindet, Bilder beschriften (S.148)

At home

bathroom · bedroom
kitchen · living room

book · lunch box
pullover · shoes

CD 2.9

1 **Listen to the CD. Draw lines.**

2 **Complete the sentences.**

The ________ are in the ________________

The _______ is in the __________________

The ____________ is in the ______________

The ______________ is in the ____________

3 **Read the sentences. Fill in the right numbers.**

1 What about playing football?

2 I like reading.

3 Watching TV is boring.

4 Do you like listening to music? – No, I don't.

5 Here's a computer game for you.

6 Do you like meeting friends? – Yes, I do.

Einen Hörtext verstehen, Sätze vervollständigen, Sätze lesen und Bildern zuordnen (S.151)

Portfolio: Free-time activities and rooms

1 What I like doing:

I like ______________________________

____

I don't like ______________________________

____

2 This is my room:

____

____

____

Freizeitaktivitäten beschreiben und illustrieren (S. 144)
das eigene Zimmer beschreiben und illustrieren (S.145)

Check your English

Ich fand die Aufgabe: ☺ leicht 😐 mittel ☹ schwer

1 Ich habe die Abbildungen auf Seite 32 durch Linien miteinander verbunde
Ich habe die Sätze vervollständigt. ☐
(Name) ____________________ und ich haben unsere Sätze verglichen und einander vorgelesen. ☐

2

☐ ☐ ☐ ☐ ☐ ☐

(Name) ____________________ und ich haben uns abwechselnd die Tätigkeiten und die Nummern dazu diktiert. ☐

3 Ich habe gefragt, was (Name) ____________________ gerne macht. ☐
Ich habe gesagt, was ich selbst mag. ☐

meeting friends ☐ watching TV ☐ playing football ☐
playing computer games ☐ listening to music ☐ reading ☐

4 Ich habe die Sätze auf Seite 32 unten gelesen und die Bilder dazu nummeriert. ☐

5 Ich habe (Name) ____________________ den Reim *Where's the cat?* aufgesagt. ☐

6 Ich habe (Name) ____________________ gesagt, wie diese Möbel heißen.

☐ ☐ ☐ ☐

__________ __________ __________ __________

Ich habe ______ Wörter richtig geschrieben.

Numbers and drinks

1 Listen to your teacher. Join the numbers.

What is it?

A ________ on a ____________________.

CD 2.12

2 Listen to the CD. Who's speaking? Tick the right answer.

3 Talk to your partner.

Do you like …?

Yes, I do.

No, I don't.

At the kiosk

apple · banana · cherry · lemon
orange · strawberry

1 Play the game.

2 Write the words.

3 Talk to a partner.

4 Write the words.

Ein Spiel spielen (S.160) · fragen, wie viel etwas kostet (S.162)

Ice cream

1 Write the words.

a banana · a cherry · a lemon · an orange · a peach

2 Write your name. Write your partner's name.
Tick your favourite ice creams.
Ask your partner.

Do you like apple ice cream?

Yes, I do.

No, I don't.

Names	apple ice cream	orange ice cream	lemon ice cream	chocolate ice cream	strawberry ice cream	vanilla ice cream	banana ice cream	cherry ice cream
My name:								
My partner's name:								

Where's my ice cream?

1 **Read the dialogues. Number the words and sentences.**

2 **Write the words and sentences.**

3 **Act it out with a partner.**

1

☐ ice cream ☐ I'm hot.

Harry: ____________________

Samir: What about some __________?

2

☐ A vanilla ☐ A strawberry

Samir: ______________ ice cream for me, please.

Kate: ______________ ice cream for me, please.

3

☐ Here you are. ☐ Thank you. ☐ Can I help you?

Woman: ____________________

Emily: Yes, I'd like some ice cream, please.

Woman: ____________________

Emily: ____________________

Harry: Where's my ice cream?
Emily: Sorry, Harry.

Eine Geschichte lesen, eine Geschichte nachspielen (S.166)

Portfolio: My favourite food and drink

1 Draw your favourite ice cream. Write about your ice cream.

My favourite ice cream is ______________________________

2 Write what food and drinks you like and don't like.

☺	☹

I like ______________________________

____

I don't like ______________________________

____

Check your English

Ich fand die Aufgabe: ☺ leicht ☹ mittel ☹ schwer

◯ CD 2.17

1 A vanilla ice cream is ______ A strawberry ice cream is ______

A lemon tea is ______ A chocolate ice cream is ______

A banana milk is ______ A cherry juice is ______

(Name) ______________________ und ich haben die Preise verglichen.
Wir haben uns gegenseitig die Sätze vorgelesen. ☐

◯

2 Diese Wörter habe ich in dem Buchstabenrätsel gefunden:

______________ ______________ ______________

______________ ______________ ______________

◯

3 Ich habe (Name) ______________________
den Reim *I eat apples* aufgesagt. ☐

◯

4 Ich habe mit (Name) ______________________ das Einkaufsgespräch gelesen und nachgespielt. ☐

◯

5 Ich habe (Name) ______________________ gefragt,
welche Eissorten er/sie mag. ☐

Ich habe (Name) ______________________ gesagt,
welche Eissorten ich mag (Seite 37). ☐

◯

6 Ich kenne noch andere Nahrungsmittel auf Englisch. ☐

____

Birthdays

1 Complete the invitation.

2 Write your answer.

party · From, Mr Mole · birthday

Dear ____________________

It's my ______________.

Can you come to my __________?

____

Thank you, I can · Sorry, I can't · Dear Mr Mole,

____

____

__________ come to your birthday party.

From, ____________________

3 Draw a present for Mr Mole. Write what it is.

My present for Mr Mole is

____

Birthdays

1 Write how old they are.

2 Number the months.

3 Write the months in the right order.

____

____

____

____

____

 Schreiben, wie alt man ist (S.175) · die Monatsnamen lesen und schreiben (S.176)

Halloween

CD 2.20

1 Listen to the CD. Write the words.

______ ______ ______ ______

______ ______ ______ ______

2 Say the words. Draw what's missing.

Halloween

Have you got a ghost on A2?

Yes, I have.

No, I haven't.

1 Cut out the ghosts on page 55. Work with your partner. Find 3 ghosts.

Partner A

Partner B

2 Write what you can see.

ghost · monster · pumpkin · skeleton · spider · witch

1  ← This is a ____________

2 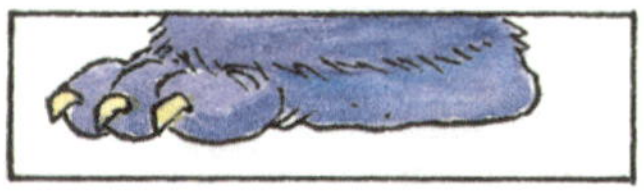
↑ This is a ____________

3 
This is a __________ →

4 
↑ This is a __________

5 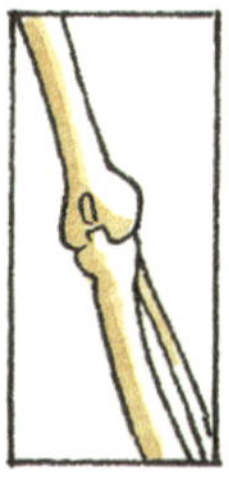
This is a ____________ →

6  ← This is a _______

What do you call a witch who lives on the beach?

A sandwitch.

Redemittel festigen, Wörter schreiben (S.180)

Christmas

CD 2.22

1 Listen to the CD. What would they like for Christmas? Draw lines.

2 Write your Christmas list.

Dear Father Christmas,

I'd like ______________________________,

______________________________,

and ______________________________

for Christmas. Thank you.

Merry Christmas!

From, ______________________________

Christmas

1 Draw lines. Write the words.

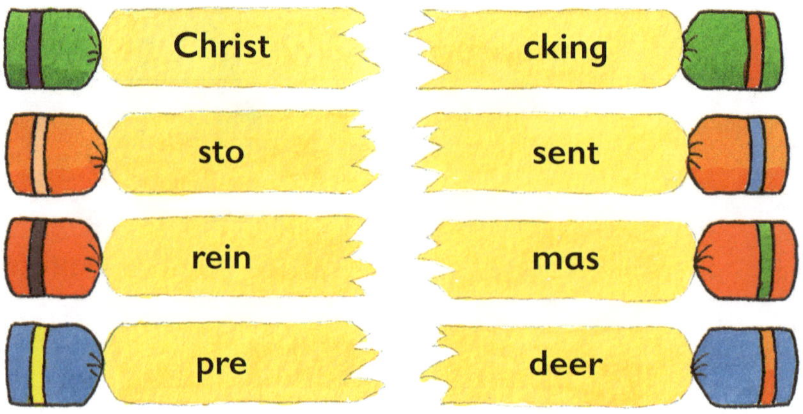

2 Write the words.

Christmas Day · Christmas Eve
Father Christmas · present · reindeer · stocking · tree

Easter

CD 2.27

1 Listen to the CD. Draw the eggs. Colour the eggs.

2 Find the words. Write the words.

Colours

Easter words

Easter

1 Read the sentences. Tick the right boxes.

	right	wrong
There's an Easter egg under the gloves.	☐	☐
There are four Easter eggs in the basket.	☐	☐
There are two Easter eggs under the skateboard.	☐	☐
There's an Easter egg behind the bunny.	☐	☐
There are three Easter eggs on the hat.	☐	☐

2 Cut out the Easter eggs on page 55. Put them on the picture. Tell your partner where they are.

Colours

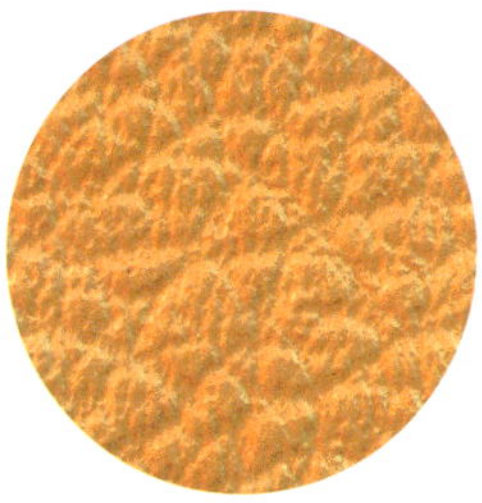

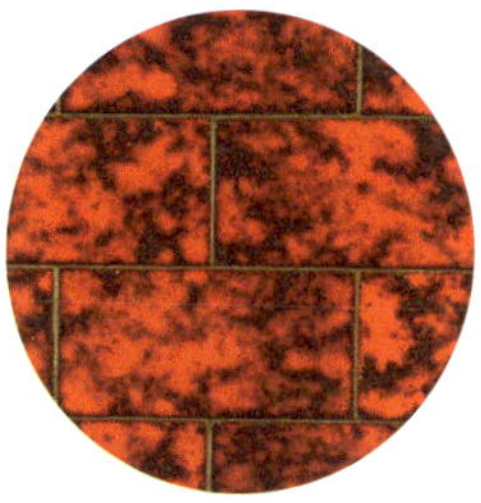

Pets

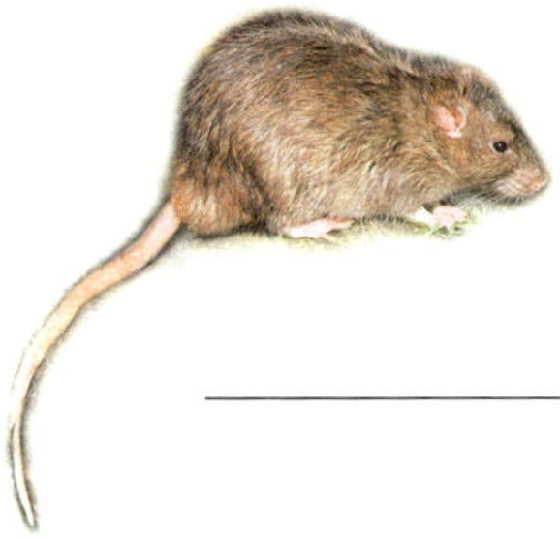

School

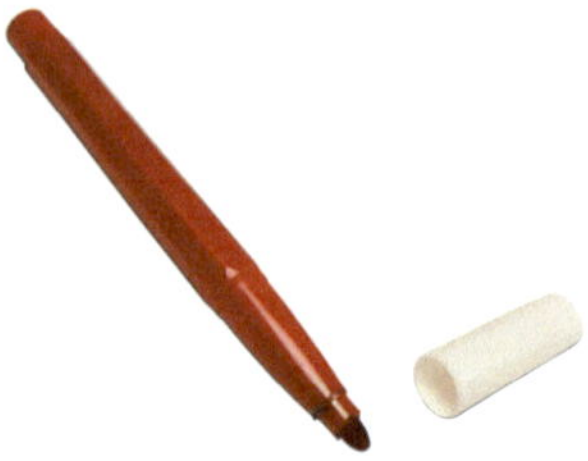

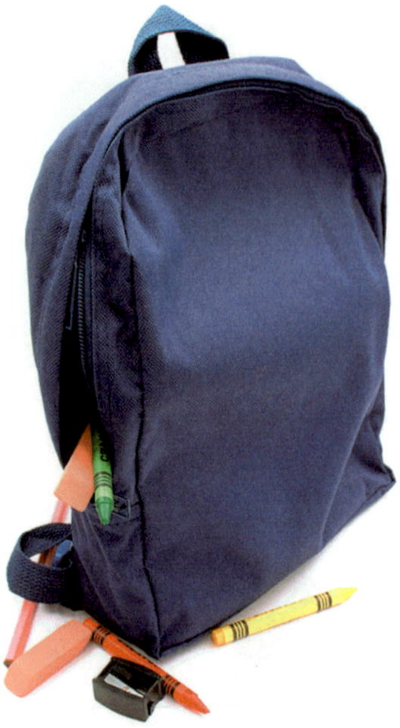

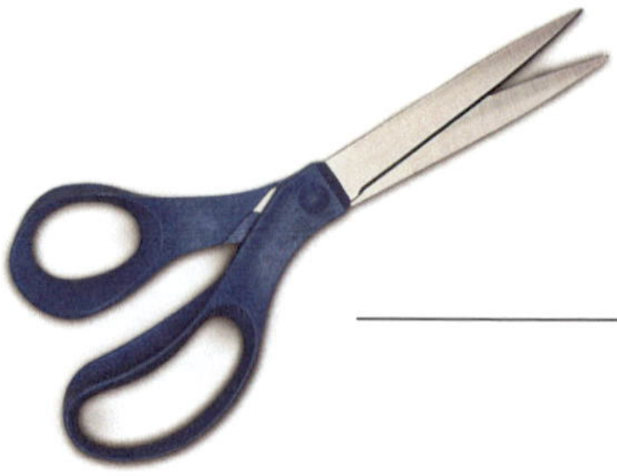

Clothes

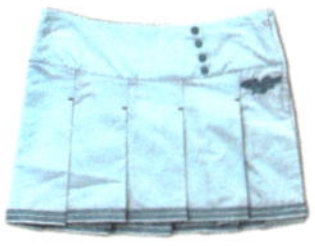

Free-time activities

Furniture

Fruit

Cut-out page

Write a card.

Page 21

Can I have your rubber, please?

Yes, you can. Here you are.

OK. Here you are.

Sorry, I haven't got a rubber.

Page 44

Page 48